Aren't These Youth?

Strategies For Helping Youth

LESLIE BLAYLARK

Aren't These Youth?

Strategies For Helping Youth

Leslie Blaylark

Table of Contents

Introduction

Ladies and gentlemen, with the deepest gratitude, I wish to thank you for listening to my humble voice. Because you could've been anywhere else in the world but you decided to be here with me. Thank you!
First and foremost, allow me to introduce myself, my name is Mr. Leslie Blaylark and just as you, I to am steady at work daily trying to better myself.
Because when a man stops learning he stops living. And, again, like yourselves, I too have much more living to do. So, allow me to ask you this question "what is your definition and description of life?" Many times, we get side tracked and fall short of our goals, due to people and events surrounding us. Influence can drain one of their purpose in life if it's the wrong influence one perceives. What I have found out was that, the hardest thing to do was to just be yourself. For whatever reason as people, we tend to give others power over us by interviewing the very thoughts of what the masses say or think of us instead of just relying on the teachings instilled within us from birth... we're taught the basic fundamentals needed to seek the truth if truth is what one is seeking.

Growing up I was surrounded by angels and a fountain of love that, to date still runneth over with abundance. I was raised by both parents under one roof so most considered me privileged. But the reality was that, first hand my parents witnessed adversity just as each young couple had during that time in ghetto America... an era of hope, dignity, and love etc. My father's father was a preacher so we knew the structure of the church. However, I also was exposed to every organized sport offered with some records still holding their own in the school books. I had a beautiful child hood. But for me it didn't seem as if it was enough, yet, I believe that I was a good kid

and like any other male child just trying to figure his own path. I reached out to what I believed as better, best... or at least I thought it was.
Everything was crazy big in the late 80's early 90's so much so, that the crack era broke the ground wide open and the abundance of many fell right thru the cracks, including myself. It was a time where the average dude became a maverick, yet, it was a time to where masses of families became separated by this new form of slavery. Fast forward 30 odd years later and other forms of activities continue to hinder the growth of our youth.
Over the years I've reflected about choices made and how influence has continued to affect the dynamics of this world. So much for being optimistic. Change is a way of life with each individual having the opportunity of its transformation. However, the essence of it all, hinders so many of us because of the foot prints before us.
What a lot of us don't realize is that, we're not of this existence to walk in the footsteps of any single person. But to learn from the experiences of others whether it be good or it be bad, because at the end of the day they don't cost us nothing their totally free to us.
I'm not here to correct you but to pass you the torch of understanding your purpose that so many have robbed you of.
History starts at this hour not tomorrow because tomorrow is not promised to neither of us. But the moment is, so capture it byway chance to change. No structure was built in one single day. But good character will last you a lifetime. So, stop looking over your shoulder at others foot prints in the sand, lace up and make your own history by being yourself and finding your purpose.
Humbly Mr. Blaylark.

Chapter 1: Understanding At-Risk Youth

Introduction

Understanding at-risk youth is crucial for developing effective strategies to support and empower them. This chapter will explore the definition of at-risk youth, the characteristics that define them, and the common factors contributing to their circumstances. By gaining insight into the unique challenges faced by these young individuals, we can better tailor our interventions to meet their needs.

Defining At-Risk Youth

At-risk youth are often defined as individuals, typically between the ages of 10 and 24, who face a higher likelihood of encountering negative outcomes due to various risk factors. These outcomes may include academic failure, substance abuse, involvement in the juvenile justice system, or mental health issues. At-risk youth may also be more vulnerable to homelessness, poverty, and social isolation.

The term "at-risk" does not imply that these youth are destined to experience negative outcomes; rather, it highlights their increased vulnerability due to their circumstances. Many at-risk youth demonstrate resilience and the capacity for positive development, given the right support and resources.

Characteristics of At-Risk Youth

At-risk youth may exhibit a range of characteristics that can inform our understanding of their unique challenges. Some of these characteristics include:

1. Academic Struggles: Many at-risk youth experience difficulties in school, such as low grades, poor attendance, and disengagement from the learning process. These challenges can stem from a lack of support at home, learning disabilities, or environmental factors.

2. Behavioral Issues: At-risk youth may display disruptive behavior, aggression, or defiance, often as a result of underlying emotional or psychological challenges. These behaviors can alienate them from peers and authority figures, exacerbating their feelings of isolation.

3. Mental Health Challenges: Mental health issues are prevalent among at-risk youth, with many experiencing anxiety, depression, trauma, or other disorders. These challenges can hinder their ability to engage socially, academically, and emotionally.

4. Substance Abuse: At-risk youth are more likely to experiment with drugs and alcohol, often as a means of coping with stress, trauma, or peer pressure. Substance abuse can have devastating effects on their physical and mental health, further complicating their situations.

5. Exposure to Violence: Many at-risk youth live in environments characterized by violence, whether in their homes, schools, or communities. Exposure to violence can lead to feelings of fear, helplessness, and a heightened sense of risk.

6. Socioeconomic Disadvantage: Poverty is a significant risk factor for youth. Economic instability can limit access to educational opportunities, healthcare, and safe recreational activities, perpetuating cycles of disadvantage.

7. Family Instability: Many at-risk youth come from families experiencing instability, such as divorce, substance abuse, or

incarceration. A lack of supportive adult figures can leave them without guidance and resources.

Common Factors Contributing to Risk

The circumstances surrounding at-risk youth are often complex and multifaceted. Several interrelated factors contribute to their increased vulnerability:

1. Environmental Factors: The community in which a youth resides plays a critical role in shaping their experiences. High-crime neighborhoods, limited access to quality schools, and a lack of recreational facilities can all contribute to feelings of hopelessness and disconnection.

2. Family Dynamics: Family is a crucial source of support and guidance for young people. Youth from families with a history of substance abuse, domestic violence, or mental health issues may struggle to develop healthy coping mechanisms and emotional resilience.

3. Educational Barriers: Many at-risk youth attend underfunded schools with limited resources. Inequities in education can lead to disengagement, lower academic achievement, and a higher likelihood of dropping out.

4. Peer Influence: Adolescents are highly influenced by their peers, and negative peer associations can lead to risky behaviors, including substance use and delinquency. Conversely, positive peer relationships can foster resilience and healthy choices.

5. Cultural and Societal Norms: Cultural expectations and societal attitudes can shape the experiences of at-risk youth. Discrimination based on race, ethnicity, gender, or sexual orientation can lead to social isolation and marginalization.

The Importance of Contextualizing At-Risk Youth

To effectively support at-risk youth, it is essential to contextualize their experiences within their individual and environmental circumstances. Each youth's journey is unique, and understanding their specific challenges, strengths, and motivations is critical to developing effective interventions.

Building Resilience

While it is important to recognize the challenges faced by at-risk youth, it is equally vital to acknowledge their resilience and capacity for growth. Many young people demonstrate remarkable strength in overcoming adversity, often drawing on personal strengths, supportive relationships, and community resources.

Strategies for fostering resilience in at-risk youth include:

1. Positive Relationships: Building trusting, supportive relationships with caring adults can provide youth with a sense of security and belonging. Mentorship programs, counseling, and community support can help nurture these connections.

2. Skill Development: Teaching life skills, coping strategies, and problem-solving techniques can empower youth to navigate challenges effectively. Programs focusing on emotional intelligence, conflict resolution, and goal-setting can be beneficial.

3. Engagement in Positive Activities: Encouraging participation in sports, arts, or community service can help at-risk youth develop a

sense of purpose, build self-esteem, and foster positive peer connections.

4. Access to Resources: Providing access to mental health services, educational support, and extracurricular opportunities can help mitigate the effects of risk factors and promote overall well-being.

Conclusion

Understanding at-risk youth requires a comprehensive examination of the defining characteristics and contributing factors to their vulnerability. By recognizing the complexities of their experiences and fostering resilience, we can create targeted strategies that empower these young individuals to thrive. The subsequent chapters will delve deeper into specific strategies and interventions, building on the foundational knowledge established in this chapter.

Chapter 2: The Role of Family Support

Introduction

Family plays a pivotal role in the development and well-being of youth, significantly influencing their behavior, emotional health, and academic success. For at-risk youth, family support can serve as a crucial protective factor that mitigates the adverse effects of various risk factors. This chapter will explore the importance of family dynamics, the types of support families can provide, strategies for engaging families in youth development, and the broader implications of fostering a supportive family environment.

Understanding Family Dynamics

1. The Family as a Foundation

The family unit is often the first social environment in which a child learns values, norms, and behaviors. A supportive family can instill resilience, self-esteem, and coping mechanisms that are vital for navigating life's challenges. Conversely, families facing dysfunction—such as abuse, neglect, or substance dependence—can create environments that contribute to the risk factors associated with youth vulnerability.

2. Types of Family Structures

Families come in various forms, including nuclear families, extended families, single-parent households, and blended families. Each structure presents unique challenges and strengths. Understanding these dynamics is essential for recognizing how they influence youth outcomes.

Nuclear Families: Typically consisting of two parents and their children, nuclear families can provide stability and consistent support. However, pressures such as financial strain or work-related stress can affect family functioning.

Single-Parent Households: These families often face challenges such as economic instability and increased stress. Single parents may struggle to provide the emotional and financial support that youth need, potentially leading to feelings of neglect or isolation.

Extended Families: In many cultures, extended families—such as grandparents, aunts, and uncles—play a significant role in child-rearing. These family members can offer additional support, guidance, and resources, creating a broader safety net for youth.

Blended Families: Families formed through remarriage or cohabitation can bring both opportunities and challenges. Youth may experience loyalty conflicts, adjustment difficulties, and varying parenting styles, impacting their emotional well-being.

The Importance of Family Support

1. Emotional Support

Emotional support from family members fosters a sense of belonging and security. Youth who feel loved, valued, and understood are more likely to develop healthy self-esteem and coping mechanisms. This emotional backing can reduce the likelihood of engaging in risky behaviors, such as substance abuse or delinquency.

2. Academic Support

Family involvement in education is critical for youth success. Parents and guardians who take an active interest in their child's academic journey—by attending school events, helping with homework, or communicating with teachers—can enhance their child's motivation and performance. Supportive family environments often lead to better educational outcomes, reduced dropout rates, and increased aspirations for higher education.

3. Social Support

Families serve as primary socialization agents, shaping youth's social skills and peer relationships. Youth with strong family support are more likely to develop positive peer relationships and healthy social networks. These relationships can serve as protective factors against the negative influences of peers.

4. Financial Support

Economic stability significantly impacts youth well-being. Families that provide financial support, whether through stable employment or community resources, can alleviate some of the stressors that contribute to youth vulnerability. Access to basic needs—such as food, clothing, and healthcare—directly affects youth's physical and emotional health.

Strategies for Engaging Families in Youth Development

1. Establishing Communication Channels

Open and effective communication is essential for engaging families in their children's development. Programs and initiatives that foster communication can empower families to participate actively in their youth's lives. Strategies include:

Regular Check-Ins: Establishing regular communication between educators, counselors, and families can keep everyone informed about a youth's progress and challenges.

Family Meetings: Creating opportunities for families to gather, share experiences, and discuss concerns can strengthen family bonds and foster a sense of community.

Utilizing Technology: Digital communication tools, such as messaging apps or online platforms, can facilitate ongoing dialogue between families and youth-serving organizations.

2. Providing Education and Resources

Educating families about the challenges their youth may face and the resources available to support them is vital. Strategies include:

Workshops and Seminars: Offering educational workshops on topics such as parenting skills, mental health awareness, and academic support can empower families to better support their youth.

Resource Guides: Developing comprehensive resource guides that outline available community services, support groups, and educational programs can help families access the help they need.

Training Programs: Providing training for families on effective communication, conflict resolution, and emotional support can enhance their ability to nurture their youth.

3. Creating Inclusive Environments

Creating environments that are welcoming and inclusive can encourage family participation in youth programs. Strategies include:
Cultural Competence: Understanding and respecting diverse family structures and cultural backgrounds can help create an inclusive atmosphere. Programs that celebrate cultural diversity and encourage family involvement can foster a sense of belonging.
Family Events: Hosting family-oriented events—such as potlucks, family nights, or community service projects—can strengthen connections between families and youth organizations.
Feedback Mechanisms: Establishing feedback channels for families to share their experiences, concerns, and suggestions can create a sense of ownership and collaboration.

Overcoming Barriers to Family Engagement

Engaging families in youth development can present challenges, particularly in high-risk environments. Common barriers include:
Time Constraints: Families may face significant time pressures due to work obligations, multiple jobs, or other responsibilities. Programs should consider flexible scheduling and virtual options to accommodate busy families.
Economic Strain: Economic hardship can limit families' ability to participate in youth programs. Offering transportation assistance, childcare services, or incentives for attendance can help mitigate these challenges.
Lack of Awareness: Some families may be unaware of the resources and programs available to support their youth. Targeted outreach efforts, community partnerships, and accessible information dissemination can help raise awareness.

The Broader Implications of Fostering Family Support

Fostering family support has far-reaching implications for both youth and communities. Strong family engagement can lead to:

Increased Resilience: Youth who feel supported by their families are more likely to develop resilience and coping strategies, enabling them to navigate challenges effectively.
Improved Community Outcomes: Engaged families contribute to healthier communities. When families are involved in youth development, they are more likely to invest in community initiatives and support positive change.
Intergenerational Impact: Supporting families can create a positive cycle that extends beyond the immediate youth population. When families receive support and resources, they can pass on those benefits to future generations, breaking cycles of disadvantage.

Conclusion

Family support is a cornerstone of healthy youth development, particularly for at-risk youth. By recognizing the importance of family dynamics, providing resources and education, and engaging families in meaningful ways, we can create a nurturing environment that empowers youth to overcome challenges and thrive. In the following chapters, we will explore additional strategies for supporting at-risk youth, building on the foundation of family engagement and involvement established in this chapter.

Chapter 3: Building Positive Relationships and Mentorship

Introduction

The relationships that at-risk youth develop with peers, adults, and mentors play a critical role in their personal growth, emotional well-being, and future success. Positive relationships can offer support, guidance, and inspiration, helping young people navigate the challenges they face. This chapter delves into the importance of building positive relationships, the role of mentorship in youth development, effective strategies for fostering these connections, and the impact of relationship-building on at-risk youth.

Understanding the Importance of Positive Relationships

1. Emotional Support and Validation

Positive relationships provide at-risk youth with emotional support, validation, and a sense of belonging. When youth feel connected to others, they are more likely to develop healthy self-esteem and resilience. This support can counteract feelings of isolation and hopelessness that often accompany at-risk circumstances.

2. Social Skills Development

Interactions with peers and adults help youth develop essential social skills, such as communication, empathy, and conflict resolution. These skills are critical for forming healthy relationships and navigating social situations. Positive role models can guide youth in developing these competencies, preparing them for future interpersonal interactions.

3. Academic and Career Guidance

Mentorship and positive relationships can significantly impact academic performance and career aspirations. Mentors can provide guidance on educational pathways, career options, and skills development, encouraging youth to pursue their goals. This guidance can lead to improved academic outcomes and increased motivation to succeed.

4. Protection Against Negative Influences

Positive relationships can serve as a buffer against negative peer pressure and risky behaviors. When at-risk youth are connected to supportive adults and peers who model healthy choices, they are less likely to engage in substance abuse, delinquency, or other harmful activities. This protective factor is especially important during adolescence, a time when peer influence is at its peak.

The Role of Mentorship in Youth Development

1. Defining Mentorship

Mentorship is a relationship in which a more experienced or knowledgeable individual provides guidance, support, and encouragement to a younger person. Mentors can serve various roles, including teacher, coach, counselor, or friend, depending on the needs of the youth and the context of the relationship.

2. The Benefits of Mentorship for At-Risk Youth

Mentorship can have profound effects on at-risk youth, including:

Increased Self-Esteem: Having a mentor can help youth feel valued and appreciated, boosting their confidence and self-worth.

Expanded Horizons: Mentors can introduce youth to new opportunities, perspectives, and experiences, broadening their worldview and aspirations.

Accountability: Mentors can help youth set goals, monitor their progress, and hold them accountable for their actions, fostering a sense of responsibility and commitment.

Skill Development: Mentors can provide practical skills training, career advice, and educational support, equipping youth with the tools they need to succeed.

3. Types of Mentoring Relationships

Mentoring can take various forms, including:

One-on-One Mentoring: A traditional model in which a single mentor works closely with a youth to provide individualized support and

guidance.
Group Mentoring: A model where a mentor works with a small group of youth, fostering peer connections and group dynamics.
Peer Mentoring: Older youth mentor younger peers, providing relatable support and guidance based on shared experiences.
Community-Based Mentoring: Mentors from the community, such as teachers, coaches, or volunteers, engage with youth outside of traditional educational settings.

Effective Strategies for Fostering Positive Relationships

1. Creating Supportive Environments

Fostering positive relationships requires creating environments where youth feel safe, respected, and valued. Strategies include:
Establishing Trust: Building trust between adults and youth is crucial. Adults should be transparent, consistent, and approachable, demonstrating their commitment to the youth's well-being.
Encouraging Open Communication: Creating spaces for open dialogue fosters honest communication. Encouraging youth to express their thoughts and feelings without fear of judgment promotes stronger relationships.
Celebrating Achievements: Recognizing and celebrating youth accomplishments, both big and small, reinforces their sense of value and belonging.

2. Training and Supporting Mentors

To maximize the impact of mentorship, it is essential to train and support mentors effectively. Strategies include:
Mentor Training Programs: Providing training on communication skills, active listening, conflict resolution, and cultural competency equips mentors with the tools they need to support youth effectively.
Regular Check-Ins: Facilitating regular check-ins between mentors and program coordinators ensures that mentors feel supported and can address challenges as they arise.

Resource Provision: Offering mentors resources and materials can enhance their ability to provide meaningful support to youth.

3. Facilitating Meaningful Connections

Creating opportunities for youth to build positive relationships is vital. Strategies include:

Structured Activities: Organizing structured activities, such as team-building exercises, community service projects, or workshops, encourages youth to connect and collaborate with peers and mentors.

Social Events: Hosting social events, such as family nights or community gatherings, fosters informal connections and strengthens community ties.

Networking Opportunities: Providing opportunities for youth to network with professionals, community leaders, and peers can expose them to new ideas and potential career pathways.

The Impact of Relationship-Building on At-Risk Youth

1. Improved Academic Performance

Youth who cultivate positive relationships with mentors and peers tend to achieve better academic outcomes. The support and guidance provided by mentors can motivate youth to engage in their studies, complete assignments, and aspire to higher education.

2. Enhanced Emotional Well-Being

Strong relationships contribute to improved emotional health for at-risk youth. Youth who feel connected to supportive adults and peers experience lower levels of anxiety and depression, fostering a greater sense of hope and resilience.

3. Reduced Risky Behaviors

Positive relationships can significantly reduce engagement in risky behaviors. Youth connected to mentors and supportive peers are less likely to engage in substance abuse, violence, or other delinquent activities.

4. Increased Civic Engagement

Mentorship fosters a sense of responsibility and community involvement among youth. As youth engage with mentors and peers, they become more likely to participate in community service, advocacy, and civic activities, contributing positively to society.

Case Studies and Success Stories

Highlighting real-life examples can illustrate the transformative power of positive relationships and mentorship for at-risk youth:

Case Study 1: The Big Brothers Big Sisters Program

The Big Brothers Big Sisters program pairs adult mentors with at-risk youth, providing one-on-one support and guidance. Studies have shown that youth involved in this program experience higher self-esteem, improved academic performance, and reduced likelihood of engaging in risky behaviors. Mentors report feeling a sense of fulfillment and purpose, creating a mutually beneficial relationship.

Case Study 2: School-Based Mentorship Programs

Many schools implement mentorship programs that connect students with older peers or community volunteers. These programs foster positive relationships and provide academic support. Schools that have adopted these initiatives report improved attendance rates, enhanced student engagement, and a more positive school climate.

Conclusion

Building positive relationships and fostering mentorship are essential strategies for supporting at-risk youth. These connections provide emotional support, guidance, and opportunities for personal growth, empowering youth to navigate challenges and achieve their potential. By creating supportive environments, training mentors, and facilitating meaningful connections, we can positively impact the lives of at-risk youth. The subsequent chapters will explore additional strategies and interventions, further contributing to the overarching goal of empowering youth to thrive despite their circumstances.

Chapter 4: Educational Interventions and Academic Support

Introduction

Education serves as a crucial foundation for the development of at-risk youth, influencing their future opportunities, self-efficacy, and life trajectories. However, many youth facing socio-economic challenges, familial instability, and other risk factors struggle in traditional educational settings. This chapter examines effective educational interventions and academic support strategies designed to empower at-risk youth. By focusing on creating supportive educational environments, implementing targeted programs, and fostering academic success, we can help at-risk youth overcome obstacles and realize their potential.

Understanding the Educational Needs of At-Risk Youth

1. Identifying At-Risk Factors

At-risk youth often experience various factors that can hinder their academic performance, including:

Socio-Economic Challenges: Economic instability can lead to issues such as hunger, homelessness, and lack of access to resources, all of which negatively affect academic success.

Family Instability: Youth from unstable family backgrounds may face challenges such as neglect, abuse, or parental substance abuse, which can significantly impact their focus and motivation in school.

Mental Health Issues: Many at-risk youth experience mental health challenges, such as anxiety, depression, or trauma-related disorders, affecting their ability to engage in the learning process.

Educational Disengagement: Students who struggle academically or feel alienated from the school environment may disengage from their education, leading to a cycle of underachievement and increased dropout rates.

2. The Importance of Addressing Educational Barriers

Recognizing and addressing these barriers is crucial for implementing effective educational interventions. Research shows that when schools and communities adopt comprehensive strategies to support at-risk youth, academic performance improves, leading to higher graduation rates and better long-term outcomes.

Effective Educational Interventions

1. Early Identification and Intervention

Early identification of at-risk youth is vital for implementing timely interventions. Schools should establish systems to monitor student performance and behavior, enabling educators to identify those in need of support quickly. Effective strategies include:

Regular Assessments: Utilizing standardized assessments and teacher observations can help identify students who may be struggling academically or socially.

Referral Systems: Developing a referral process for teachers and staff to connect at-risk youth with support services can facilitate early intervention.

2. Tailored Academic Support Programs

Tailored academic support programs can address the specific needs of at-risk youth, enhancing their educational experience. Key strategies include:

Tutoring Programs: Providing one-on-one or small-group tutoring can help struggling students catch up with their peers. Peer tutoring programs, where older students assist younger ones, can also foster positive relationships and boost confidence.

After-School Programs: After-school programs that offer homework help, enrichment activities, and mentorship can provide additional support for at-risk youth. These programs can create a safe space for youth to engage in learning outside of traditional school hours.

Individualized Education Plans (IEPs): For youth with learning disabilities or special needs, developing IEPs that outline specific goals and accommodations can facilitate academic success.

3. Social and Emotional Learning (SEL)

Incorporating Social and Emotional Learning (SEL) into the educational curriculum can significantly benefit at-risk youth. SEL focuses on developing essential life skills, including emotional regulation, interpersonal skills, and decision-making. Effective strategies include:

SEL Curriculum: Implementing a structured SEL curriculum can teach students to manage emotions, build relationships, and set goals. Schools can integrate these lessons into existing subjects or offer dedicated SEL classes.

Restorative Practices: Utilizing restorative practices to address conflict and behavior issues fosters a positive school culture. These practices encourage dialogue, understanding, and accountability, promoting healthier relationships among students and staff.

Fostering Supportive Educational Environments

1. Creating Inclusive Classrooms

Inclusive classrooms that celebrate diversity and accommodate various learning styles foster a sense of belonging for at-risk youth. Effective strategies include:

Differentiated Instruction: Teachers should employ differentiated instruction techniques to tailor lessons to individual learning needs. This approach ensures that all students, regardless of ability, can access the curriculum and succeed.

Culturally Responsive Teaching: Incorporating culturally relevant materials and perspectives into lessons can help at-risk youth see themselves reflected in their education. This practice fosters engagement and motivation among diverse student populations.

2. Engaging Families in Education

Family engagement is crucial for supporting at-risk youth academically. Strategies to involve families include:

Parent-Teacher Conferences: Schools should regularly hold parent-teacher conferences to discuss student progress and strategies for support. Creating a welcoming environment encourages family participation.

Family Literacy Programs: Offering family literacy programs can help parents improve their own education while empowering them to support their children's learning. These programs can include workshops on academic support, communication, and involvement in school activities.

The Role of Community Partnerships

1. Collaborating with Community Organizations

Partnerships with local organizations can enhance educational support for at-risk youth. Community resources can provide additional services, mentorship, and opportunities for engagement. Strategies include:

Internships and Job Shadowing: Collaborating with local businesses to offer internships and job shadowing opportunities can expose youth to various career paths and build professional skills.

Service Learning Projects: Engaging youth in service-learning projects promotes civic responsibility and provides real-world learning experiences. These projects can help youth connect academic concepts to their communities.

2. Mental Health Support Services

Integrating mental health support services within educational settings is essential for addressing the emotional and psychological needs of at-risk youth. Strategies include:

On-Site Counseling Services: Schools can partner with mental health organizations to provide on-site counseling for students,

ensuring they have access to necessary support.
Training Staff on Mental Health Awareness: Educating teachers and staff about mental health issues and how to recognize signs of distress can promote a supportive school environment.

The Impact of Educational Interventions

1. Improved Academic Outcomes

Research consistently shows that effective educational interventions lead to improved academic performance among at-risk youth. Programs that provide personalized support and address barriers to learning result in higher grades, increased graduation rates, and greater aspirations for post-secondary education.

2. Enhanced Social Skills

Educational interventions that focus on social and emotional learning contribute to the development of essential life skills. At-risk youth who engage in SEL programs often demonstrate improved interpersonal skills, better conflict resolution abilities, and increased emotional regulation.

3. Increased Graduation Rates

Comprehensive support for at-risk youth can significantly impact graduation rates. Schools that implement effective interventions report lower dropout rates and a higher percentage of students successfully completing their high school education.

Case Studies and Success Stories

Case Study 1: The Success of the Harlem Children's Zone

The Harlem Children's Zone (HCZ) is a comprehensive community initiative that provides a range of educational and support services to children and families in Harlem. HCZ employs a holistic approach, offering early childhood education, tutoring, mentorship, and health services. As a result, HCZ has seen significant improvements in student achievement, with many youth progressing to college and successful careers.

Case Study 2: The Power of After-School Programs

Research has shown that students who participate in high-quality after-school programs experience improved academic performance and increased engagement in school. Programs that offer academic support, enrichment activities, and mentorship have proven particularly effective for at-risk youth, providing a safe and nurturing environment for learning.

Conclusion

Educational interventions and academic support are critical for empowering at-risk youth and helping them overcome barriers to success. By implementing tailored programs, fostering supportive educational environments, and engaging families and community partners, we can create a framework that promotes academic achievement, personal growth, and resilience. The following chapters will continue to explore additional strategies for supporting at-risk youth, building on the foundation established in this chapter and reinforcing the importance of education in their journey toward success.

Chapter 5: Mentoring and Relationship Building

Introduction

Mentoring and building strong, supportive relationships are essential strategies for helping at-risk youth navigate the challenges they face. Research indicates that positive relationships with caring adults can significantly impact a young person's development, improving their social skills, self-esteem, and academic performance. This chapter explores the importance of mentoring and relationship building in the lives of at-risk youth, outlines effective mentoring programs, and discusses the critical role that adults—parents, educators, and community members—play in fostering positive relationships.

Understanding the Importance of Mentoring

1. Defining Mentorship

Mentorship is a dynamic, reciprocal relationship between a mentor and a mentee, characterized by guidance, support, and encouragement. Mentors can be teachers, coaches, family members, or community leaders who provide their mentees with advice, resources, and personal experiences to help them navigate life's challenges.

2. The Benefits of Mentorship for At-Risk Youth

Mentoring has proven benefits for at-risk youth, including:

Enhanced Academic Performance: Mentored youth often experience improved academic outcomes. Mentors provide academic support, encouragement, and accountability, helping mentees stay focused on their studies.

Increased Self-Esteem and Confidence: Mentoring relationships foster a sense of belonging and validation. When mentors believe in their mentees, it can enhance their self-esteem and confidence, motivating them to pursue their goals.

Improved Social Skills: Mentoring can help youth develop critical social skills, such as communication, teamwork, and conflict resolution. These skills are essential for building healthy relationships and succeeding in various social contexts.
Expanded Networks and Opportunities: Mentors often introduce their mentees to new experiences, perspectives, and professional networks. These connections can open doors for internships, job opportunities, and additional resources.

Building Effective Mentoring Programs

1. Designing a Mentoring Program

Successful mentoring programs require careful planning and structure. Key components to consider include:
Clear Goals and Objectives: Establishing specific goals for the mentoring program helps ensure that both mentors and mentees understand their roles and expectations. Goals should focus on academic achievement, personal development, and social skills enhancement.
Targeted Recruitment of Mentors: Identifying and recruiting mentors who are committed, compassionate, and culturally competent is critical. Mentors should reflect the diversity of the mentees they serve and possess skills and experiences relevant to the challenges youth face.
Comprehensive Training for Mentors: Providing training and resources for mentors equips them with the tools they need to effectively support their mentees. Training should cover topics such as active listening, communication skills, and recognizing signs of distress in youth.
Ongoing Support and Supervision: Establishing a system of ongoing support and supervision for mentors ensures they feel connected to the program and can seek assistance when needed. Regular check-ins and feedback opportunities can help maintain mentor engagement.

2. Matching Mentors and Mentees

Effective matching of mentors and mentees is crucial for fostering a strong mentoring relationship. Considerations for matching include:

Shared Interests and Backgrounds: Pairing mentors and mentees with similar interests or backgrounds can enhance rapport and trust. When mentees see aspects of themselves in their mentors, they may feel more comfortable sharing their experiences and challenges.

Personality Compatibility: Assessing the personalities of both mentors and mentees can help create harmonious matches. Using personality assessments or informal interviews can guide the matching process.

Availability and Commitment: Ensuring that both mentors and mentees have the time and commitment to engage in the relationship is essential. Clear expectations regarding time commitments should be established from the outset.

3. Structure and Activities in Mentoring Relationships

Providing a structure for mentoring sessions can enhance the effectiveness of the relationship. Mentoring activities can include:

Regular Meetings: Establishing a consistent schedule for meetings—whether weekly, biweekly, or monthly—ensures that mentors and mentees maintain regular contact and build a trusting relationship over time.

Goal Setting: Mentors and mentees should collaboratively set goals to guide their discussions and activities. These goals can be academic, personal, or skill-based, providing focus and motivation.

Engaging Activities: Incorporating engaging activities into mentoring sessions can strengthen the relationship while fostering skill development. Activities may include:

Academic Support: Reviewing schoolwork or preparing for tests together can enhance the mentee's academic skills.

Life Skills Development: Engaging in discussions about life skills, such as time management, goal setting, and problem-solving, can

provide practical tools for success.
Community Involvement: Participating in community service projects together can foster a sense of civic responsibility and create shared experiences.

The Role of Educators in Mentorship

1. Teacher-Student Mentorship

Teachers can play a significant role in mentoring at-risk youth within the school setting. Strategies for fostering teacher-student mentorship include:
Creating a Supportive Classroom Environment: Teachers can establish a welcoming and inclusive classroom environment that encourages open communication and relationship building.
Individualized Attention: Providing individualized attention to students can help teachers identify their unique needs and strengths, fostering deeper connections.
Advisory Programs: Implementing advisory programs where teachers serve as advisors to a small group of students can create opportunities for mentorship and support outside the traditional classroom setting.

2. Professional Development for Educators

Investing in professional development for educators enhances their mentoring abilities. Training should focus on:
Cultural Competence: Educators should receive training in cultural competence to better understand and connect with their diverse student populations.
Trauma-Informed Practices: Educators equipped with trauma-informed practices can provide better support for at-risk youth who have experienced trauma, fostering a safe and understanding environment.

The Role of Family in Building Relationships

1. Engaging Families in Mentoring

Family involvement is crucial for the success of mentoring relationships. Strategies to engage families include:

Family Orientation Sessions: Hosting orientation sessions for families can inform them about the mentoring program's goals, processes, and benefits, fostering a sense of community and collaboration.

Encouraging Family Participation: Providing opportunities for families to participate in mentoring activities—such as family nights or workshops—can strengthen connections and support youth development.

2. Enhancing Parent-Mentor Relationships

Encouraging collaboration between parents and mentors can create a supportive network for at-risk youth. Strategies include:

Regular Communication: Establishing regular communication between mentors and parents can keep families informed about their child's progress and challenges.

Collaborative Goal Setting: Involving parents in the goal-setting process ensures that the goals align with the family's values and aspirations for their child.

Community Involvement in Mentoring

1. Partnering with Community Organizations

Collaboration with community organizations can enhance mentoring programs by providing additional resources and support. Effective strategies include:

Leveraging Local Resources: Partnering with local businesses, nonprofits, and government agencies can provide mentors with resources, training, and funding to support their work with at-risk youth.

Connecting with Volunteer Networks: Engaging with volunteer networks and community service organizations can expand the pool of potential mentors and provide a diverse range of experiences and perspectives.

2. Creating a Mentoring Culture in the Community

Fostering a culture of mentoring within the community can create a supportive environment for at-risk youth. Strategies to promote a mentoring culture include:

Community Awareness Campaigns: Launching awareness campaigns to highlight the importance of mentoring and encourage community members to get involved can build momentum for mentoring initiatives.

Mentoring Events: Organizing community events that celebrate mentoring relationships and provide information about local mentoring programs can attract new mentors and mentees.

Measuring the Impact of Mentoring

1. Evaluation of Mentoring Programs

Regular evaluation of mentoring programs is essential for assessing their effectiveness and making necessary adjustments. Key evaluation components include:

Data Collection: Collecting qualitative and quantitative data on mentee outcomes—such as academic performance, attendance rates, and social-emotional development—can provide insights into the program's impact.

Feedback from Participants: Gathering feedback from mentors, mentees, and families can help identify strengths and areas for improvement within the program.

2. Success Stories and Impact Assessments

Highlighting success stories of at-risk youth who have benefited from mentoring can inspire others and demonstrate the program's impact. Successful case studies can include:

Graduation Successes: Sharing stories of mentees who have graduated high school or pursued higher education can illustrate the power of mentorship in transforming lives.

Personal Growth: Documenting mentees' personal growth, increased self-confidence, and improved social skills can provide compelling evidence of the program's benefits.

Conclusion

Mentoring and relationship building are essential components of supporting at-risk youth. By fostering positive relationships, establishing effective mentoring programs, and involving families and communities, we can create a network of support that empowers youth to overcome challenges and thrive. This chapter emphasizes the transformative power of mentorship in shaping the lives of at-risk youth and underscores the responsibility of educators, families, and community members to engage in meaningful relationships that foster growth and resilience. The following chapters will explore additional strategies for helping at-risk youth, further expanding on the foundations laid in this chapter.

Chapter 6: Community Engagement and Support Systems

Introduction

Community engagement and the establishment of robust support systems are fundamental strategies for helping at-risk youth. Communities play a critical role in shaping the experiences and outcomes of young people, and when they come together to support their youth, they create a powerful network that can foster resilience, growth, and opportunity. This chapter will delve into the importance of community engagement, the various forms it can take, and the establishment of support systems that ensure at-risk youth have the resources and encouragement they need to thrive.

Understanding Community Engagement

1. Defining Community Engagement

Community engagement involves the active participation of individuals and organizations within a community to address issues, share resources, and collaborate towards common goals. It fosters a sense of belonging, shared responsibility, and collective action, which are essential for promoting the well-being of youth.

2. The Importance of Community Engagement for At-Risk Youth

Engaging the community in support of at-risk youth can lead to numerous benefits, including:

Increased Resources and Opportunities: When communities unite to support youth, they can pool resources, knowledge, and skills to create more opportunities for engagement, education, and personal development.

Strengthened Relationships: Community engagement fosters relationships among families, schools, local organizations, and youth, creating a safety net that youth can rely on during challenging times.

Empowerment and Ownership: Involving community members in programs and initiatives empowers them to take ownership of their environment, increasing their investment in the well-being of youth.
Reduction of Isolation: Many at-risk youth experience feelings of isolation or disconnection. Community engagement helps counteract this by fostering a sense of belonging and support.

Building a Community Network

1. Identifying Key Stakeholders

To build an effective community network, it is crucial to identify and engage key stakeholders, including:
Schools and Educational Institutions: Schools are often at the forefront of addressing the needs of at-risk youth. Collaborating with educators can enhance academic support and outreach efforts.
Nonprofits and Community Organizations: Local nonprofits can offer programs, resources, and expertise in youth development and support. Forming partnerships with these organizations can enrich community initiatives.
Faith-Based Organizations: Many faith-based organizations provide support to youth and families, offering mentoring, after-school programs, and resources for personal development.
Local Businesses: Engaging local businesses can lead to sponsorships, internships, and job opportunities for youth. Businesses can also contribute to community initiatives through funding or in-kind donations.

2. Creating Collaborative Initiatives

Collaborative initiatives can help mobilize resources and expertise within the community. Effective strategies include:
Community Advisory Boards: Establishing advisory boards composed of community members, educators, parents, and youth can ensure that programs are responsive to the needs of at-risk

youth. These boards can provide guidance and feedback on initiatives.

Resource Fairs and Workshops: Organizing resource fairs that connect youth and families with local services—such as mental health support, job training, and educational opportunities—can enhance community engagement.

Youth-Led Initiatives: Encouraging youth to take leadership roles in community initiatives can empower them and provide them with valuable skills. Youth-led projects can focus on issues they are passionate about, fostering a sense of agency and responsibility.

Developing Support Systems

1. Understanding Support Systems

Support systems for at-risk youth encompass a range of services and resources designed to promote their well-being and success. These systems can be formal or informal and should involve collaboration among families, schools, community organizations, and mental health services.

2. The Components of Effective Support Systems

To create an effective support system for at-risk youth, consider the following components:

Mental Health Services: Access to mental health resources is essential for addressing the emotional and psychological needs of at-risk youth. Schools can collaborate with mental health providers to offer counseling services, workshops, and support groups.

Academic Support Services: Providing tutoring, homework help, and mentorship programs can help youth succeed academically. After-school programs that focus on educational enrichment can also enhance learning opportunities.

Social Services: Connecting youth and families with social services—such as housing assistance, food security programs, and financial literacy resources—can address the systemic barriers that often contribute to at-risk behavior.

Recreational Opportunities: Engaging youth in recreational and extracurricular activities can foster positive social interactions, improve physical health, and enhance overall well-being. Sports leagues, arts programs, and youth clubs can provide safe spaces for youth to connect and grow.

Strategies for Enhancing Community Engagement

1. Raising Awareness

Increasing awareness of the challenges faced by at-risk youth is essential for garnering community support. Strategies for raising awareness include:

Community Forums and Discussions: Hosting forums where community members can discuss the needs and concerns of at-risk youth can foster understanding and encourage collective action.

Public Campaigns: Utilizing social media, local news outlets, and community events to share stories of at-risk youth and highlight the importance of community support can mobilize resources and volunteers.

2. Mobilizing Volunteers

Recruiting and training volunteers is a vital part of building community support for at-risk youth. Effective strategies include:

Volunteer Recruitment Drives: Organizing recruitment drives at schools, community centers, and local businesses can help identify potential volunteers who are passionate about supporting youth.

Training Programs: Providing training for volunteers ensures they are equipped with the skills and knowledge necessary to effectively support youth. Topics may include active listening, youth development, and cultural competence.

Establishing Sustainable Programs

1. Creating Long-Term Partnerships

Sustainability is key to the success of community initiatives supporting at-risk youth. Considerations for creating long-term partnerships include:
Memorandums of Understanding (MOUs): Formal agreements between organizations can outline shared goals, responsibilities, and resources, ensuring commitment from all parties involved.
Regular Evaluation and Feedback: Establishing mechanisms for ongoing evaluation and feedback allows organizations to assess the effectiveness of their programs and make necessary adjustments for continuous improvement.

2. Securing Funding and Resources
To ensure the sustainability of support systems, organizations must secure funding and resources. Strategies for funding include:
Grant Applications: Actively seeking grants from local, state, and federal sources can provide necessary funding for community programs. Collaborating with experienced grant writers can enhance success rates.
Fundraising Events: Organizing community fundraising events can raise awareness and generate financial support. Events can include charity runs, auctions, and community festivals.

Measuring Success and Impact
1. Developing Evaluation Metrics
Establishing clear metrics for evaluating the success of community engagement and support systems is crucial. Considerations for developing metrics include:
Youth Outcomes: Measuring improvements in academic performance, mental health, and social skills among at-risk youth can help assess the effectiveness of programs.
Community Involvement: Tracking community participation in initiatives and volunteer hours can indicate the level of engagement and support for at-risk youth.

Feedback from Participants: Collecting feedback from youth, families, and community members can provide valuable insights into the strengths and weaknesses of programs.

2. Celebrating Success Stories

Highlighting and celebrating success stories can inspire others and demonstrate the impact of community engagement. Strategies include:

Spotlighting Achievements: Recognizing the accomplishments of at-risk youth, such as academic achievements or personal growth, can motivate others and encourage continued support.

Sharing Stories: Utilizing local media and social media platforms to share stories of positive change and resilience among at-risk youth can inspire community involvement.

Conclusion

Community engagement and the establishment of robust support systems are critical strategies for helping at-risk youth overcome challenges and reach their full potential. By mobilizing resources, fostering collaboration among stakeholders, and ensuring access to essential services, communities can create a supportive environment that empowers youth to thrive. This chapter emphasizes the importance of collective action and highlights the transformative impact that a united community can have on the lives of at-risk youth. The following chapters will continue to explore additional strategies for supporting at-risk youth, building upon the foundation of community engagement and support systems.

Chapter 7: Mentorship and Role Models

Introduction

Mentorship and positive role models play a pivotal role in the development of at-risk youth. Through guidance, encouragement, and the provision of valuable life skills, mentors can help young people navigate the complexities of adolescence and emerge as resilient, capable individuals. This chapter explores the significance of mentorship, the characteristics of effective mentors, and various mentorship models and programs that can be implemented to support at-risk youth.

The Importance of Mentorship

1. Defining Mentorship

Mentorship is a supportive relationship in which an experienced individual (the mentor) provides guidance, advice, and encouragement to a less experienced person (the mentee). Mentorship can occur in various settings, including schools, community organizations, and informal relationships, and can significantly impact the lives of at-risk youth.

2. Benefits of Mentorship for At-Risk Youth

Mentorship offers numerous benefits to at-risk youth, including:

Emotional Support: Mentors can provide a safe space for youth to express their feelings, discuss challenges, and develop coping strategies. This emotional support is crucial for fostering resilience and self-esteem.

Skill Development: Mentors can help youth develop essential life skills, such as communication, problem-solving, and decision-making. These skills are vital for academic and personal success.

Exposure to Opportunities: Mentors can introduce youth to new experiences, opportunities, and networks, broadening their horizons and encouraging them to pursue their goals.

Accountability: A mentor can help youth set goals and hold them accountable for their progress. This accountability can motivate youth to stay focused and committed to their personal development.
Positive Role Models: By providing positive examples of behavior, mentors can influence the values and attitudes of at-risk youth, encouraging them to make healthier choices.

Characteristics of Effective Mentors

1. Building Trust and Rapport

Effective mentors are skilled at building trust and rapport with their mentees. They create an environment where youth feel safe to express themselves and share their concerns. Key strategies for building trust include:
Active Listening: Mentors should practice active listening, demonstrating genuine interest in their mentee's thoughts and feelings. This approach fosters open communication and strengthens the mentor-mentee relationship.
Empathy: Demonstrating empathy allows mentors to understand their mentee's perspective and experiences, validating their feelings and creating a supportive environment.

2. Commitment and Consistency

Mentors must be committed to their mentees and the mentoring process. This commitment involves:
Regular Meetings: Establishing a consistent schedule for meetings or interactions is essential. Regular engagement fosters continuity and strengthens the relationship.
Availability: Mentors should be accessible and willing to provide support when needed. Being available for emergencies or unexpected challenges reinforces the mentor's commitment.

3. Setting Boundaries and Expectations

Effective mentors establish clear boundaries and expectations within the mentoring relationship. This clarity helps to define the roles and responsibilities of both the mentor and mentee, contributing to a healthy and productive partnership. Key considerations include:
Goal Setting: Mentors should work with their mentees to set realistic and achievable goals, ensuring that both parties understand what they aim to accomplish.
Respecting Privacy: Mentors must respect the privacy of their mentees, creating a safe space for sharing without fear of judgment or breach of confidentiality.

Mentorship Models and Programs

1. One-on-One Mentoring

One-on-one mentoring involves a single mentor providing guidance and support to one mentee. This model allows for personalized attention and tailored guidance, catering to the unique needs of the youth. Key components include:
Individualized Approach: Mentors can focus on the specific challenges and goals of their mentees, creating a customized plan for growth and development.
Building Stronger Relationships: One-on-one interactions allow for deeper connections and trust to develop between mentors and mentees.

2. Group Mentoring

Group mentoring involves a mentor working with a small group of youth. This model can be effective in fostering peer support and encouraging collaboration among participants. Benefits include:
Peer Learning: Group mentoring promotes peer learning and sharing of experiences, allowing youth to benefit from diverse perspectives and insights.

Social Skill Development: Engaging in group activities helps youth develop social skills, teamwork, and communication abilities.

3. Peer Mentoring

Peer mentoring involves youth mentoring their peers, often with the guidance of an adult facilitator. This model leverages the relatability of peers, making it a powerful tool for at-risk youth. Key elements include:

Shared Experiences: Peer mentors can connect with their mentees on a personal level, sharing similar experiences and challenges.

Empowerment: Peer mentoring empowers youth by placing them in a position of responsibility, encouraging leadership and confidence.

4. Community-Based Mentoring Programs

Community-based mentoring programs are structured initiatives that connect youth with mentors from the community. These programs often involve partnerships with schools, nonprofits, and local organizations. Key considerations include:

Structured Framework: Community-based programs typically provide a structured framework for mentorship, including training for mentors, clear objectives, and regular evaluations.

Diverse Mentor Pool: These programs often draw on a diverse pool of mentors from various backgrounds, offering youth a range of perspectives and experiences.

Implementing a Mentorship Program

1. Program Development

Developing an effective mentorship program requires careful planning and consideration of the specific needs of at-risk youth. Key steps include:

Needs Assessment: Conducting a needs assessment to identify the unique challenges faced by at-risk youth in the community can

inform program design and focus.
Goal Setting: Establishing clear goals for the mentorship program helps define its purpose and the desired outcomes for participants.

2. Recruitment and Training of Mentors
Recruiting and training mentors is a critical aspect of program implementation. Strategies include:
Targeted Recruitment: Actively recruiting mentors from diverse backgrounds, including professionals, community leaders, and college students, can enhance the program's impact.
Training Workshops: Providing training workshops for mentors ensures they are equipped with the skills and knowledge necessary to support at-risk youth effectively. Topics may include communication strategies, cultural competence, and conflict resolution.

3. Matching Mentors and Mentees
The matching process is crucial for the success of the mentorship relationship. Considerations include:
Shared Interests and Goals: Matching mentors and mentees based on shared interests, backgrounds, and goals can enhance compatibility and rapport.
Ongoing Support: Providing ongoing support and resources for mentors and mentees throughout the relationship can help address challenges and reinforce the mentoring process.

Evaluating Mentorship Programs
1. Assessment Metrics
Evaluating the effectiveness of mentorship programs is essential for understanding their impact and areas for improvement. Metrics may include:

Youth Development: Assessing changes in academic performance, social skills, and self-esteem among mentees can provide insight into the program's effectiveness.
Mentor Satisfaction: Gathering feedback from mentors regarding their experiences and challenges can inform future training and support efforts.

2. Continuous Improvement

Establishing a culture of continuous improvement ensures that mentorship programs adapt to changing needs and feedback. Strategies include:
Regular Evaluations: Conducting regular evaluations of program outcomes and participant feedback can inform necessary adjustments and enhancements.
Incorporating Feedback: Actively incorporating feedback from mentors and mentees into program design and implementation can foster a responsive and effective mentoring environment.

Success Stories and Case Studies

1. Highlighting Impact

Sharing success stories and case studies can illustrate the positive impact of mentorship on at-risk youth. Examples may include:
Academic Achievement: Highlighting mentees who have improved their academic performance or pursued higher education can inspire others and showcase the effectiveness of mentorship.
Personal Growth: Documenting personal growth stories, such as increased self-esteem or improved social skills, can demonstrate the transformative power of mentorship.

Conclusion

Mentorship and positive role models are essential strategies for helping at-risk youth overcome challenges and develop the skills needed for success. By fostering supportive relationships, providing guidance, and exposing youth to new opportunities, mentors can significantly impact the lives of young people. This chapter has highlighted the importance of mentorship, the characteristics of effective mentors, and various mentorship models that can be implemented to support at-risk youth. As we continue to explore strategies for helping at-risk youth, the subsequent chapters will delve into additional approaches that complement the mentoring process and further promote positive outcomes.

Chapter 8: Creating Safe Spaces

Introduction

Creating safe spaces is essential for at-risk youth to thrive and develop positively. These spaces foster an environment where young people feel secure, valued, and respected, allowing them to explore their identities, express themselves, and engage in healthy relationships. This chapter delves into the concept of safe spaces, their significance for at-risk youth, the elements that contribute to a safe environment, and practical strategies for creating and maintaining these spaces.

Understanding Safe Spaces

1. Definition of Safe Spaces

A safe space is an environment where individuals can feel free from discrimination, harassment, and judgment. In the context of at-risk youth, safe spaces provide a sanctuary where they can express their thoughts and feelings without fear of negative repercussions. These spaces can be physical locations, such as community centers or schools, or virtual environments, such as online support groups and forums.

2. Importance of Safe Spaces for At-Risk Youth

The importance of safe spaces for at-risk youth cannot be overstated. These environments offer numerous benefits, including:

Emotional Safety: Safe spaces allow youth to express their emotions and vulnerabilities without fear of ridicule or criticism. This emotional safety is crucial for developing self-esteem and resilience.

Open Communication: In safe spaces, young people can engage in open and honest discussions about their experiences, challenges, and aspirations. This open communication fosters trust and builds a sense of community.

Empowerment: Safe spaces empower youth to take control of their narratives and advocate for themselves. By providing a platform for their voices to be heard, these spaces encourage self-advocacy and agency.

Social Connection: Safe spaces promote social connections among youth, helping them form friendships and support networks. These connections can be vital for their emotional well-being and overall development.

Elements of a Safe Space

1. Inclusivity and Diversity

Creating an inclusive environment that celebrates diversity is essential for establishing a safe space. Key components include:

Cultural Sensitivity: Recognizing and respecting the diverse backgrounds, cultures, and identities of youth is crucial. Programs should promote cultural sensitivity and inclusivity by incorporating diverse perspectives into activities and discussions.

Non-Discrimination Policies: Establishing and enforcing clear non-discrimination policies helps create a culture of acceptance and respect. These policies should address issues related to race, gender, sexual orientation, ability, and other factors that may contribute to marginalization.

2. Physical Environment

The physical environment of a safe space plays a significant role in its overall effectiveness. Considerations include:

Comfortable and Welcoming Atmosphere: The space should be inviting and comfortable, with age-appropriate furnishings and decor that reflect the interests of youth. Creating a visually appealing environment can enhance youth engagement and participation.

Safety and Accessibility: Ensuring the physical safety and accessibility of the space is paramount. This includes addressing any safety concerns, such as proper lighting and security measures, as well as making the space accessible for individuals with disabilities.

3. Supportive Staff and Mentors

The presence of supportive staff and mentors is critical in fostering a safe environment. Elements to consider include:

Trained Personnel: Staff members and mentors should be trained in trauma-informed practices, cultural competency, and conflict resolution. This training equips them with the skills necessary to support at-risk youth effectively.

Approachability: Staff and mentors should be approachable and relatable to youth, creating a sense of trust and comfort. Building rapport with young people encourages them to seek help and guidance when needed.

4. Clear Rules and Boundaries

Establishing clear rules and boundaries helps create a structured environment that promotes safety and respect. Key considerations include:

Behavior Expectations: Setting clear expectations for behavior helps define acceptable and unacceptable actions within the space. These expectations should be communicated to all participants and reinforced consistently.

Conflict Resolution Protocols: Implementing conflict resolution protocols can help address issues that arise in the space. These protocols should emphasize open communication, mediation, and restorative practices.

Strategies for Creating Safe Spaces

1. Involve Youth in the Process

Engaging youth in the creation and maintenance of safe spaces is essential for fostering a sense of ownership and investment.

Strategies include:
Youth Leadership Opportunities: Providing opportunities for youth to take on leadership roles within the space empowers them to influence the environment positively. Youth-led committees or focus groups can help shape programming and policies.
Feedback Mechanisms: Establishing feedback mechanisms allows youth to share their thoughts and suggestions regarding the space. Regular check-ins and surveys can help assess their needs and preferences.

2. Offer Training and Workshops

Providing training and workshops on topics related to safe spaces can equip both youth and staff with the skills needed to maintain a supportive environment. Key topics may include:
Conflict Resolution: Training youth in conflict resolution strategies can empower them to address disagreements constructively and promote a harmonious atmosphere.
Mental Health Awareness: Workshops on mental health awareness can help youth recognize and address their emotional needs, fostering a culture of support and understanding.

3. Foster Community Partnerships

Collaborating with community organizations can enhance the resources and support available within safe spaces. Considerations include:
Resource Sharing: Partnering with local mental health organizations, educational institutions, and youth service agencies can provide additional resources, such as counseling services, educational programs, and workshops.
Community Events: Organizing community events that promote inclusion and celebrate diversity can strengthen relationships among

youth, families, and community members, further enhancing the safe space's impact.

Case Studies of Successful Safe Spaces

1. Community Youth Center

A community youth center established a safe space for at-risk youth by incorporating the following elements:

Inclusive Programming: The center offered diverse programming that addressed the interests and needs of youth from various backgrounds. Activities included art workshops, mentorship programs, and educational support.

Youth Leadership Council: A youth leadership council was formed to give participants a voice in decision-making processes. This council provided valuable feedback on programming and helped create a sense of ownership within the center.

Trained Staff: The center employed trained staff members who were committed to fostering a supportive environment. Regular training sessions on cultural competency and trauma-informed care ensured that staff were equipped to address the diverse needs of youth.

2. School-Based Safe Spaces

A local high school implemented a safe space initiative aimed at supporting LGBTQ+ students. Key components included:

Gender-Neutral Facilities: The school created gender-neutral bathrooms and changing facilities to promote inclusivity and respect for all students.

Safe Zone Training: Staff members participated in safe zone training to become allies for LGBTQ+ students, fostering an environment of acceptance and understanding.

Support Groups: The school established support groups for LGBTQ+ youth, providing a platform for students to connect, share experiences, and access resources.

Challenges in Creating Safe Spaces

1. Resistance to Change

Establishing safe spaces may face resistance from various stakeholders, including parents, school administration, or community members. Strategies to address this challenge include:

Education and Awareness: Providing education about the importance of safe spaces and their benefits can help alleviate concerns and build support among stakeholders.

Engaging Stakeholders: Involving parents, community members, and school administration in discussions about safe spaces can foster collaboration and reduce resistance.

2. Sustainability

Ensuring the long-term sustainability of safe spaces can be challenging, especially in terms of funding and resources. Key strategies include:

Grant Writing and Fundraising: Seeking grants and engaging in fundraising efforts can help secure financial support for safe space initiatives.

Community Support: Building strong community partnerships can enhance resource availability and promote a collaborative approach to maintaining safe spaces.

Conclusion

Creating safe spaces for at-risk youth is a vital strategy for fostering positive development and emotional well-being. By establishing inclusive, supportive, and empowering environments, we can help youth navigate the challenges they face and develop the skills necessary for success. This chapter has explored the concept of safe spaces, the elements that contribute to their effectiveness, and practical strategies for implementation. As we move forward, subsequent chapters will address additional strategies that complement the creation of safe spaces, further enhancing the support available to at-risk youth.

Chapter 9: Life Skills Development

Introduction

Life skills development is a foundational component in the journey of at-risk youth toward achieving personal growth, self-sufficiency, and overall well-being. These skills encompass a range of competencies necessary for managing daily life, making informed decisions, and effectively navigating social interactions. For at-risk youth, developing life skills can significantly reduce vulnerability to negative outcomes, such as dropping out of school, engaging in risky behaviors, or becoming involved in the juvenile justice system. This chapter delves into the importance of life skills development, identifies essential skills for youth, explores effective teaching methods, and provides real-world examples of successful programs.

The Importance of Life Skills for At-Risk Youth

1. Building Resilience and Independence

Life skills are crucial for fostering resilience and independence among at-risk youth. When young people learn to manage their emotions, set goals, and solve problems, they become better equipped to handle life's challenges. This resilience empowers them to make positive choices, resist peer pressure, and adapt to new situations, leading to improved mental health and self-esteem.

2. Enhancing Employability

In today’s competitive job market, possessing strong life skills is often as important as academic qualifications. Employers increasingly seek individuals who can communicate effectively, work collaboratively, and demonstrate critical thinking. By developing these skills, at-risk youth enhance their employability and increase their chances of securing stable, rewarding employment.

3. Promoting Healthy Relationships

Life skills development also plays a vital role in fostering healthy relationships. Skills such as communication, empathy, and conflict resolution enable youth to build and maintain positive connections with peers, family members, and authority figures. Healthy relationships, in turn, provide essential support systems that contribute to overall well-being.

4. Supporting Academic Success

Life skills are closely linked to academic success. Youth who develop effective study habits, time management skills, and goal-setting abilities are more likely to perform well in school. Furthermore, life skills education can help students navigate challenges such as bullying, stress, and academic pressure, reducing dropout rates and promoting educational attainment.

Essential Life Skills for At-Risk Youth

1. Communication Skills

Effective communication is a critical life skill that encompasses both verbal and non-verbal interactions. Key components include: Active Listening: The ability to listen attentively and respond appropriately to others fosters mutual understanding and respect.

Expressing Emotions: Teaching youth how to articulate their feelings and needs can enhance self-awareness and improve interpersonal relationships.

Conflict Resolution: Skills in conflict resolution enable youth to address disagreements constructively, reducing the likelihood of escalation and fostering peaceful interactions.

2. Decision-Making and Problem-Solving Skills

The ability to make informed decisions and solve problems is essential for navigating life's challenges. Key aspects include:

Analyzing Options: Teaching youth to assess different options and consider potential outcomes fosters critical thinking and responsible decision-making.

Weighing Consequences: Helping youth understand the consequences of their choices encourages them to think ahead and make decisions aligned with their goals and values.

Developing Solutions: Problem-solving skills empower youth to identify solutions to challenges, enhancing their confidence and independence.

3. Financial Literacy

Financial literacy is a crucial skill that prepares youth for future financial responsibilities. Key components include: Budgeting: Teaching youth how to create and manage a budget helps them understand the importance of tracking income and expenses. Saving and Investing: Educating youth about saving strategies and the basics of investing can promote long-term financial security. Understanding Credit: Providing insights into credit scores, loans, and responsible borrowing equips youth to make informed financial decisions.

4. Goal-Setting and Time Management

Goal-setting and time management are essential for achieving personal and academic success. Key aspects include: SMART Goals: Teaching youth to set Specific, Measurable, Achievable, Relevant, and Time-bound (SMART) goals encourages them to clarify their aspirations and develop actionable plans. Prioritization: Helping youth prioritize tasks and manage their time effectively enhances productivity and reduces stress. Monitoring Progress: Encouraging youth to track their progress toward goals fosters accountability and reinforces a growth mindset.

5. Self-Care and Emotional Regulation

Self-care and emotional regulation skills are crucial for maintaining mental health and well-being. Key components include: Stress Management: Teaching youth stress management techniques, such as mindfulness and relaxation exercises, equips them to cope with life's pressures. Recognizing Triggers: Helping youth identify emotional triggers and develop coping strategies promotes emotional awareness and

resilience.
Seeking Help: Encouraging youth to seek help when needed fosters a proactive approach to mental health and well-being.

Effective Teaching Methods for Life Skills Development

1. Experiential Learning

Experiential learning emphasizes hands-on, real-world experiences that engage youth in the learning process. Strategies include: Role-Playing: Engaging youth in role-playing scenarios can help them practice communication and conflict resolution skills in a safe environment.
Simulations: Financial literacy programs can incorporate simulations, such as managing a virtual budget, to provide practical experience in money management.
Community Projects: Involving youth in community service projects fosters collaboration, problem-solving, and social responsibility while allowing them to apply their skills in meaningful contexts.

2. Interactive Workshops

Interactive workshops promote active participation and encourage skill-building through group activities. Key components include:
Group Discussions: Facilitating discussions on relevant topics allows youth to share their experiences and learn from one another.
Games and Challenges: Incorporating games and challenges into workshops can make learning fun while reinforcing essential life skills.
Guest Speakers: Inviting guest speakers from various professions can expose youth to diverse perspectives and inspire them to envision future possibilities.

3. Mentorship and Peer Support

Mentorship and peer support are invaluable for life skills development. Considerations include:

Peer Mentoring: Pairing youth with peer mentors who have successfully navigated similar challenges can provide relatable guidance and support.

Mentor Training: Training mentors to facilitate life skills development ensures that they have the tools and knowledge to effectively support their mentees.

Support Groups: Establishing support groups for at-risk youth creates a safe space for sharing experiences, challenges, and successes.

Real-World Examples of Life Skills Development Programs

1. The 4-H Youth Development Program

The 4-H program, a national initiative in the United States, focuses on experiential learning and life skills development for youth. Key components include: Hands-On Projects: Youth engage in hands-on projects, such as gardening, cooking, and animal care, fostering a range of life skills.

Leadership Development: 4-H emphasizes leadership development through opportunities for youth to take on leadership roles in their clubs and communities.

Positive Outcomes: Research shows that participants in 4-H programs demonstrate higher levels of leadership skills, communication skills, and community engagement compared to their peers.

2. Boys & Girls Clubs of America

The Boys & Girls Clubs of America provide a safe and supportive environment for youth to develop essential life skills. Key components include: Life Skills Programming: Clubs offer life skills programming focused on topics such as financial literacy, health and wellness, and conflict resolution.

Mentorship Opportunities: Youth are paired with adult mentors who provide guidance and support in their personal and academic lives. Community Engagement: Clubs encourage youth to engage in community service projects, fostering a sense of social responsibility and teamwork.

Challenges in Life Skills Development

1. Resistance to Learning

At-risk youth may exhibit resistance to learning life skills due to various factors, including past negative experiences or lack of motivation. Strategies to address this challenge include: Building Trust: Establishing trust between educators and youth is essential for creating a supportive learning environment.

Relating to Interests: Tailoring life skills development to align with the interests and passions of youth can enhance engagement and motivation.

2. Resource Limitations

Limited resources, such as funding and trained personnel, can hinder the implementation of life skills programs. Considerations include: Community Partnerships: Collaborating with local organizations, schools, and businesses can help secure resources and support for life skills programs.

Grant Opportunities: Pursuing grant opportunities can provide funding for life skills development initiatives.

Conclusion

Life skills development is a critical strategy for empowering at-risk youth and promoting their overall well-being and success. By focusing on essential skills such as communication, decision-making, financial literacy, and emotional regulation, we can equip youth with the tools they need to navigate life's challenges and build a brighter future. Through effective teaching methods and real-world examples of successful programs, we can create impactful life skills development initiatives that foster resilience, independence, and positive outcomes for at-risk youth. In the following chapters, we will continue to explore additional strategies for helping at-risk youth, ensuring a holistic approach to their development and success.

Chapter 10: Addressing Substance Abuse

Introduction

Substance abuse among youth is a pervasive issue that has far-reaching consequences for individuals, families, and communities. At-risk youth are particularly vulnerable to substance use due to various factors, including environmental influences, peer pressure, trauma, and mental health challenges. This chapter aims to provide a comprehensive understanding of substance abuse among at-risk youth, explore the underlying causes, discuss effective prevention and intervention strategies, and highlight successful programs that have made a positive impact.

Understanding Substance Abuse

1. Definition and Scope

Substance abuse refers to the harmful or hazardous use of psychoactive substances, including alcohol, illicit drugs, and prescription medications. According to the Substance Abuse and Mental Health Services Administration (SAMHSA), approximately 18% of adolescents aged 12 to 17 reported using illicit drugs in the past year, and 10% reported binge drinking. The rates of substance abuse are particularly alarming among marginalized populations and those living in high-risk environments.

2. Types of Substances Commonly Abused

Alcohol: The most commonly abused substance among youth, alcohol consumption can lead to a range of negative consequences, including academic failure, risky behavior, and addiction.

Marijuana: Often perceived as a "soft" drug, marijuana use is prevalent among youth and can impact cognitive development, motivation, and mental health.

Stimulants: Drugs such as cocaine and methamphetamine are associated with increased risk for addiction and can lead to severe

health issues.
Prescription Drugs: Opioids, benzodiazepines, and stimulants are frequently misused by youth, often obtained from family members or friends.
Inhalants: Common household products like glue, paint thinners, and aerosol sprays are sometimes used for their psychoactive effects, posing serious health risks.

Causes of Substance Abuse in At-Risk Youth

1. Environmental Factors

Family Dynamics: Youth from families with a history of substance abuse are at a higher risk of developing similar patterns. Dysfunctional family environments characterized by conflict, neglect, or lack of parental supervision contribute significantly to substance use.
Socioeconomic Status: Low socioeconomic status is often linked to limited access to education, healthcare, and recreational opportunities, increasing vulnerability to substance abuse.
Peer Pressure: Adolescents are highly influenced by their peers, and the desire to fit in or gain acceptance can lead to experimentation with drugs and alcohol.

2. Mental Health Issues

Co-occurring Disorders: Many at-risk youth struggle with mental health disorders such as depression, anxiety, and trauma-related disorders, which can lead to self-medication through substance use.
Emotional Regulation: Difficulty in managing emotions can push youth toward substances as a coping mechanism to escape negative feelings.

3. Trauma and Adverse Childhood Experiences (ACEs)

Trauma Exposure: Youth who have experienced trauma, including abuse, neglect, or exposure to violence, are at an increased risk for substance abuse as they seek to numb emotional pain or cope with distressing memories.

Adverse Childhood Experiences: ACEs, such as household dysfunction, parental substance abuse, and poverty, can have a cumulative impact on a youth's likelihood of developing substance use disorders.

Prevention Strategies

1. Education and Awareness Programs

School-Based Education: Implementing comprehensive substance abuse prevention programs in schools can educate students about the risks associated with drug and alcohol use. Topics may include the effects of substances on physical and mental health, the importance of making informed choices, and skills for resisting peer pressure.

Community Awareness Campaigns: Local communities can organize campaigns to raise awareness about substance abuse, targeting parents, youth, and educators to foster a collective understanding of the issue.

2. Strengthening Family Support

Parenting Programs: Providing resources and training for parents to enhance their parenting skills can strengthen family dynamics and reduce the likelihood of substance abuse. Programs may focus on communication, discipline strategies, and building healthy relationships.

Family Therapy: Involving families in therapy can address underlying issues, improve communication, and support youth in developing healthy coping mechanisms.

3. Building Resilience and Social Skills

Life Skills Training: Teaching youth essential life skills, such as decision-making, stress management, and problem-solving, can empower them to resist substance use and navigate challenges more effectively.

Positive Peer Relationships: Encouraging youth to engage in healthy peer relationships through extracurricular activities, sports, and clubs can provide supportive social networks that reduce the likelihood of substance use.

Intervention Strategies

1. Early Identification and Screening

Routine Screening: Implementing regular screenings for substance use in schools and healthcare settings can help identify at-risk youth early on, allowing for timely intervention.

Training for Educators: Training teachers and school staff to recognize signs of substance abuse and understand the appropriate referral processes can facilitate early identification and support.

2. Counseling and Support Services

Individual Counseling: Providing access to trained counselors who can offer individual therapy for youth struggling with substance abuse is essential. Counselors can address underlying mental health issues, trauma, and substance use behaviors.

Group Therapy: Group therapy settings can foster a sense of community among youth facing similar challenges. This environment allows for sharing experiences, gaining support, and learning coping strategies from peers.

3. Treatment Programs

Outpatient Treatment: For youth with less severe substance use issues, outpatient treatment programs can provide flexibility and support while allowing them to remain in their home environment.

Inpatient Rehabilitation: For those with severe addiction, inpatient rehabilitation programs offer intensive support, structure, and therapeutic interventions necessary for recovery.

Successful Programs Addressing Substance Abuse

1. SMART Recovery

SMART Recovery (Self-Management and Recovery Training) is a peer-support program that provides resources and tools for individuals dealing with substance use disorders. The program emphasizes self-empowerment, goal setting, and cognitive-behavioral strategies to promote recovery. Key components include:

Facilitated Meetings: Participants engage in group meetings led by trained facilitators, where they learn practical skills for managing their recovery.

Educational Resources: SMART Recovery offers various resources, including worksheets, online forums, and a comprehensive website, to support participants in their journey to recovery.

2. The Partnership for Drug-Free Kids

The Partnership for Drug-Free Kids is a national organization that provides resources and support for families dealing with substance abuse. Key components include:

Helpline Services: The organization offers a confidential helpline for parents to seek guidance on navigating their child's substance use issues.

Education and Awareness: The Partnership provides educational materials to help families understand the signs of substance abuse and strategies for prevention and intervention.

Challenges in Addressing Substance Abuse

1. Stigma and Shame

Stigma surrounding substance abuse can deter youth and their families from seeking help. It is crucial to create an environment that fosters open dialogue and reduces shame associated with substance use.

2. Access to Resources

Limited access to treatment resources, particularly in underserved communities, poses a significant barrier to addressing substance abuse. Advocacy for increased funding and support for substance abuse programs is essential.

3. Continuity of Care

Ensuring continuity of care post-treatment is critical for long-term recovery. Establishing connections between treatment programs and ongoing support services can help youth maintain their recovery and prevent relapse.

Conclusion

Addressing substance abuse among at-risk youth requires a multifaceted approach that encompasses prevention, early identification, intervention, and ongoing support. By understanding the underlying causes of substance use, implementing effective prevention strategies, and providing comprehensive intervention programs, we can empower youth to overcome challenges, build resilience, and achieve long-term recovery. As we continue to explore additional strategies for helping at-risk youth in the following chapters, it is vital to recognize the critical role that addressing substance abuse plays in fostering healthier, more successful futures for our young people.

Chapter 11: Promoting Positive Peer Relationships

Introduction

Positive peer relationships play a pivotal role in the emotional and social development of youth, especially for those at risk. At-risk youth often face numerous challenges, including social isolation, exposure to negative influences, and emotional difficulties. Building and maintaining healthy peer relationships can serve as a protective factor, promoting resilience, enhancing self-esteem, and reducing the likelihood of engaging in risky behaviors. This chapter delves into the importance of positive peer relationships, explores strategies for fostering these connections, and highlights successful programs that have made significant strides in supporting youth development through peer engagement.

The Importance of Positive Peer Relationships

1. Social Development

Peer relationships provide youth with essential social experiences that contribute to their emotional and psychological growth. Engaging with peers helps youth learn critical social skills, including communication, conflict resolution, and empathy. These skills are vital for navigating relationships in adulthood and contribute to overall well-being.

2. Emotional Support

Positive peer relationships offer emotional support during challenging times. Friends provide a sense of belonging, understanding, and validation, which can be especially crucial for at-risk youth dealing with trauma, mental health issues, or family problems. Emotional support from peers can mitigate feelings of isolation and anxiety, fostering resilience.

3. Reduced Risk of Negative Behaviors

Healthy peer relationships can act as a protective factor against negative behaviors such as substance abuse, delinquency, and other risky activities. When youth are surrounded by positive influences, they are less likely to engage in harmful behaviors. Conversely, negative peer associations can lead to poor decision-making and increased vulnerability to risky situations.

4. Enhancing Self-Esteem

Positive interactions with peers contribute to higher self-esteem and self-worth. When youth feel accepted and valued by their peers, they are more likely to develop a positive self-image. This self-esteem can translate into academic success, improved mental health, and a greater likelihood of pursuing positive life goals.

Factors Influencing Peer Relationships

1. Environmental Influences

Family Dynamics: The family environment significantly influences youth's ability to form positive peer relationships. Supportive, communicative families foster youth's confidence in social situations, while dysfunctional families may hinder social development.

Community Context: Communities characterized by safety, inclusivity, and accessible resources provide youth with opportunities to engage with peers positively. Conversely, communities marked by violence, discrimination, or limited recreational opportunities can negatively impact youth's social interactions.

2. Individual Characteristics

Personality Traits: Individual personality traits, such as extroversion or introversion, can influence the types of peer relationships youth form. Extroverted youth may find it easier to connect with others, while introverted youth may require more support to engage socially.

Social Skills: The ability to communicate effectively, empathize with others, and navigate social situations plays a crucial role in establishing and maintaining positive peer relationships. Youth with well-developed social skills are better equipped to form meaningful connections.

3. Cultural and Societal Factors

Cultural Norms: Different cultures may have varying expectations regarding friendships and social interactions. Understanding these cultural nuances is essential for fostering inclusive environments where all youth feel comfortable building relationships.

Peer Group Dynamics: Peer group dynamics, including the influence of popular or dominant groups, can shape individual youth's behavior and choices. Encouraging youth to engage with diverse peer groups can promote positive interactions and broaden social experiences.

Strategies for Promoting Positive Peer Relationships

1. Building Social Skills

Social Skills Training: Implementing programs that teach essential social skills can equip youth with the tools they need to build positive relationships. Skills such as active listening, effective communication, and conflict resolution should be emphasized.

Role-Playing Activities: Engaging youth in role-playing scenarios can help them practice social interactions in a safe environment. This approach allows youth to explore different social situations and develop their confidence in real-life interactions.

2. Creating Opportunities for Peer Interaction

Extracurricular Activities: Schools and community organizations should provide diverse extracurricular activities, such as sports, arts, and clubs, where youth can engage with peers who share similar interests. These settings facilitate natural interactions and relationship-building.

Peer Mentoring Programs: Establishing peer mentoring programs can create structured opportunities for youth to connect positively.

Older students or trained peers can serve as mentors, guiding younger individuals in navigating social situations and building friendships.

3. Encouraging Inclusivity and Diversity

Diverse Group Activities: Creating group activities that promote diversity and inclusivity can encourage youth from different backgrounds to interact and form connections. Emphasizing teamwork and collaboration can help break down social barriers.

Anti-Bullying Initiatives: Implementing anti-bullying programs that foster a culture of respect and acceptance can create safer environments for youth to engage with one another. Education on empathy and understanding differences is crucial in promoting positive relationships.

4. Facilitating Open Communication

Safe Spaces for Dialogue: Creating safe spaces for youth to discuss their feelings and experiences can foster deeper connections. Group discussions, support circles, or facilitated dialogues can provide youth with opportunities to share and listen to one another.

Parental Involvement: Encouraging open communication between parents and youth about friendships and social interactions can provide valuable support. Parents should be educated on the importance of fostering healthy peer relationships and how to facilitate positive connections.

Successful Programs Promoting Positive Peer Relationships

1. The Buddy System

The Buddy System is an innovative program that pairs students with peers who may be new to the school, experiencing social anxiety, or struggling with relationship-building. Key components of the program include:

Pairing Mechanism: Students are paired based on interests, backgrounds, or specific needs, creating a structured yet flexible environment for social engagement.
Regular Check-ins: Facilitators conduct regular check-ins to monitor the progress of buddy pairs, providing support and guidance as needed.
Group Activities: The program includes group activities that encourage buddy pairs to collaborate, fostering friendship and trust.

2. Peer Leadership Programs
Peer Leadership Programs empower youth to take on leadership roles within their schools and communities. These programs train youth to serve as positive role models and mentors to their peers. Key components include:
Leadership Training: Participants receive training on leadership skills, effective communication, and conflict resolution, equipping them to guide others.
Community Service Projects: Peer leaders engage in community service projects that promote teamwork and collaboration while positively impacting their communities.
Workshops on Inclusivity: Workshops that emphasize inclusivity and empathy help peer leaders understand the importance of fostering positive relationships among their peers.

Challenges in Promoting Positive Peer Relationships
1. Overcoming Negative Peer Influences
At-risk youth may be influenced by negative peer groups that promote harmful behaviors. Developing strategies to help youth recognize and navigate these influences is essential for promoting positive relationships.
2. Addressing Social Anxiety and Isolation
Some youth may struggle with social anxiety or have difficulty connecting with peers, leading to feelings of isolation. Tailored

interventions that provide support for these individuals can help them build confidence and develop social skills.

3. Ensuring Inclusivity

Fostering an inclusive environment requires ongoing effort and commitment from educators, parents, and community members. Addressing systemic biases and discrimination is crucial in promoting positive peer relationships among diverse youth.

Conclusion

Promoting positive peer relationships is a vital component of supporting at-risk youth's social and emotional development. By understanding the significance of peer interactions, identifying the factors influencing relationships, and implementing effective strategies and programs, we can create environments that empower youth to build healthy connections. As we continue to explore additional strategies for helping at-risk youth in the following chapters, we must recognize the transformative power of positive peer relationships in shaping their futures and fostering resilience in the face of adversity.

Chapter 12: Engaging Youth in Decision-Making

Introduction

Engaging youth in decision-making processes is essential for fostering a sense of ownership, responsibility, and empowerment among young individuals, particularly those at risk. When youth are actively involved in decisions that affect their lives and communities, they are more likely to develop critical thinking skills, improve their self-esteem, and foster a sense of agency. This chapter explores the importance of youth engagement in decision-making, identifies strategies for facilitating meaningful participation, and highlights successful programs that exemplify best practices in youth engagement.

The Importance of Engaging Youth in Decision-Making

1. Empowerment and Agency

Engaging youth in decision-making empowers them to take charge of their lives and instills a sense of agency. When young individuals are involved in making decisions, they are more likely to feel valued and respected, leading to increased confidence and self-efficacy. Empowered youth are better equipped to navigate challenges and advocate for their needs and rights.

2. Development of Critical Skills

Participation in decision-making processes helps youth develop essential life skills, including critical thinking, problem-solving, and communication. These skills are vital for success in various aspects of life, including education, employment, and personal relationships. By actively engaging in discussions and deliberations, youth learn to analyze information, weigh options, and articulate their perspectives.

3. Increased Commitment to Outcomes

When youth are involved in the decision-making process, they are more likely to commit to the outcomes of those decisions. Their involvement fosters a sense of ownership and accountability, motivating them to work towards achieving the goals set forth. This commitment can lead to more effective implementation of programs and initiatives, as youth take pride in their contributions.

4. Representation of Diverse Perspectives

Youth engagement in decision-making ensures that diverse perspectives are represented in discussions and policy-making. At-risk youth often have unique experiences and insights that can inform better practices and policies. By including youth voices, decision-makers can develop more comprehensive and effective solutions that address the needs of the community.

Factors Influencing Youth Engagement

1. Socioeconomic Context

The socioeconomic context in which youth live can significantly influence their ability to engage in decision-making. Youth from lower-income backgrounds may face barriers such as limited access to resources, education, and supportive networks that can hinder their participation. Addressing these systemic barriers is crucial for fostering equitable engagement opportunities.

2. Educational Environment

The educational environment plays a vital role in shaping youth engagement. Schools that promote a culture of inclusivity, respect, and collaboration are more likely to encourage student participation in decision-making processes. Conversely, rigid or authoritarian educational environments may stifle youth voices and discourage engagement.

3. Community Support

Supportive community structures and organizations can facilitate youth engagement in decision-making. Access to mentors, programs, and resources that promote civic involvement can empower youth to participate actively in their communities. Collaborative partnerships between schools, families, and community organizations are essential for creating a supportive ecosystem for youth engagement.

Strategies for Engaging Youth in Decision-Making

1. Creating Opportunities for Participation

Youth Advisory Councils: Establishing youth advisory councils can provide structured opportunities for youth to engage in decision-making. These councils should represent diverse perspectives and be given a genuine platform to voice their opinions on relevant issues.

Participatory Workshops: Hosting participatory workshops that invite youth to share their thoughts and ideas on specific topics fosters an inclusive environment. These workshops can utilize creative methods such as brainstorming sessions, role-playing, and group discussions to encourage engagement.

2. Educating Youth about Decision-Making Processes

Workshops on Civic Engagement: Educating youth about civic engagement and the decision-making process is crucial for empowering them to participate effectively. Workshops that cover topics such as local governance, advocacy, and community organizing can enhance their understanding and skills.

Leadership Training Programs: Implementing leadership training programs equips youth with the skills and knowledge needed to navigate decision-making processes. These programs can include training on effective communication, negotiation, and conflict resolution.

3. Encouraging Youth-Led Initiatives

Youth-Driven Projects: Supporting youth-led projects allows young individuals to take the lead in decision-making and implementation. Providing resources and mentorship for these initiatives fosters a sense of ownership and responsibility.

Grant Opportunities for Youth Initiatives: Establishing grant opportunities specifically for youth-led initiatives encourages young individuals to develop and implement projects that address community needs. This funding can support innovative ideas and empower youth to create positive change.

4. Promoting Collaborative Partnerships

Collaboration with Community Organizations: Building partnerships with community organizations can enhance youth engagement in decision-making. These organizations can provide resources, mentorship, and support, creating a network that amplifies youth voices.

Involvement of Families: Engaging families in the decision-making process fosters a supportive environment for youth. Providing opportunities for families to participate in discussions and decisions related to youth initiatives can strengthen connections and enhance overall engagement.

Successful Programs Promoting Youth Engagement

1. The Youth Empowerment Program

The Youth Empowerment Program (YEP) focuses on engaging young individuals in community decision-making processes. Key components include:

Community Forums: YEP organizes community forums where youth can voice their opinions on local issues, propose solutions, and engage in discussions with community leaders.

Capacity-Building Workshops: Workshops that enhance leadership skills and civic knowledge empower youth to participate actively in decision-making.

Mentorship Opportunities: YEP pairs youth with mentors who guide them through the decision-making process and help them develop their advocacy skills.

2. Youth Action Networks

Youth Action Networks bring together young individuals from diverse backgrounds to collaborate on community projects and initiatives. Key components of these networks include:

Collaborative Projects: Youth work together on projects that address specific community needs, allowing them to practice decision-making skills in a real-world context.

Peer Leadership: Youth leaders within the network guide their peers, fostering a culture of collaboration and empowerment.

Feedback Mechanisms: The network incorporates feedback mechanisms that allow youth to reflect on their experiences and make improvements to future initiatives.

Challenges in Engaging Youth in Decision-Making

1. Systemic Barriers

Systemic barriers, such as socioeconomic disparities and lack of access to resources, can hinder youth engagement in decision-making processes. Addressing these barriers requires comprehensive efforts at the community and policy levels to create equitable opportunities for all youth.

2. Resistance from Authority Figures

Resistance from authority figures, such as educators or community leaders, can stifle youth engagement. Overcoming this resistance requires building trust and demonstrating the value of youth perspectives in decision-making processes.

3. Lack of Awareness or Knowledge

Some youth may lack awareness of their rights or knowledge of how to engage in decision-making. Providing education and resources that promote understanding of civic engagement is crucial for empowering youth to participate effectively.

Conclusion

Engaging youth in decision-making processes is a critical strategy for empowering at-risk individuals and fostering their development. By creating opportunities for participation, educating youth about decision-making, encouraging youth-led initiatives, and promoting collaborative partnerships, we can cultivate a generation of informed, engaged, and empowered young individuals. As we continue to explore additional strategies for helping at-risk youth in the subsequent chapters, it is essential to recognize the transformative impact of youth engagement on their lives and communities. By valuing their voices and contributions, we pave the way for a brighter future for all.

Chapter 14: Evaluating Program Effectiveness

Introduction

Effective evaluation of programs designed to assist at-risk youth is critical for ensuring that interventions are impactful, relevant, and sustainable. Evaluation provides insights into what works, what doesn't, and why. It helps organizations allocate resources effectively, demonstrate accountability to stakeholders, and drive continuous improvement. This chapter explores the importance of evaluating program effectiveness, outlines various evaluation frameworks and methodologies, and discusses the key components of a comprehensive evaluation plan.

The Importance of Program Evaluation

1. Ensuring Accountability and Transparency

Program evaluation fosters accountability by providing stakeholders —such as funders, community members, and policymakers—with evidence of program effectiveness. Transparency in evaluation allows organizations to share successes and challenges openly, building trust within the community and among stakeholders.

2. Informed Decision-Making

Evaluation provides data that inform decision-making at all levels of an organization. By understanding the strengths and weaknesses of a program, leaders can make informed decisions about resource allocation, program modifications, and potential scaling or replication of successful initiatives.

3. Continuous Improvement

Evaluating program effectiveness is an ongoing process that supports continuous improvement. Regular evaluation allows organizations to refine their strategies, adapt to changing circumstances, and better meet the needs of the youth they serve. This iterative process fosters innovation and responsiveness, which are essential in addressing the complex challenges facing at-risk youth.

4. Demonstrating Impact

Effective evaluation allows organizations to demonstrate their impact on youth outcomes. By collecting and analyzing data, organizations can show how their programs contribute to positive changes in areas such as academic achievement, mental health, social skills, and overall well-being. This evidence can be powerful in advocating for continued funding and support.

Evaluation Frameworks and Methodologies

1. Logic Model

A logic model is a visual representation that outlines the relationships between program resources, activities, outputs, and outcomes. It serves as a roadmap for evaluation, helping stakeholders understand how program components work together to achieve desired outcomes.

Components of a Logic Model:

Inputs: The resources invested in the program, including funding, staff, materials, and partnerships.

Activities: The specific actions and interventions implemented in the program, such as workshops, mentoring, or counseling sessions.

Outputs: The measurable products of the program activities, such as the number of participants served or sessions conducted.

Outcomes: The short-term, intermediate, and long-term changes expected as a result of the program, such as improved academic performance or enhanced coping skills.

2. Theory of Change

A theory of change provides a detailed explanation of how and why a program is expected to produce specific outcomes. It outlines the causal pathways and assumptions underlying the program's design, helping stakeholders understand the rationale behind the chosen interventions.

Key Elements of a Theory of Change:

Context: The environmental factors and conditions that influence the program.

Interventions: The strategies and activities employed to achieve change.

Outcomes: The expected changes in participants resulting from the interventions.

Assumptions: The beliefs about how and why the program will lead to desired outcomes.

3. Mixed Methods Approach

A mixed methods approach combines qualitative and quantitative evaluation techniques to provide a comprehensive understanding of program effectiveness. This approach allows evaluators to gather numerical data (quantitative) while also capturing the experiences and perspectives of participants (qualitative).

Quantitative Methods: Surveys, assessments, and standardized tests that measure specific outcomes and provide statistical data on program effectiveness.

Qualitative Methods: Interviews, focus groups, and observations that offer insights into participant experiences, program implementation, and contextual factors influencing outcomes.

Key Components of a Comprehensive Evaluation Plan 1. Defining Evaluation Goals and Questions

The first step in developing an evaluation plan is to define the goals of the evaluation and formulate specific questions that the evaluation seeks to answer. Clear goals and questions guide the evaluation process and ensure that the focus remains on key areas of interest.

Example Goals:

Assess the impact of a mentoring program on youth academic performance.
Evaluate the effectiveness of a substance abuse prevention initiative.

Example Questions:
To what extent did participants improve their academic grades after participating in the mentoring program?
What changes in attitudes toward substance use were observed among participants in the prevention initiative?

2. Identifying Data Sources and Collection Methods Data collection methods should be aligned with the evaluation goals and questions. It is essential to identify relevant data sources, including participant surveys, pre- and post-assessments, program attendance records, and qualitative feedback from interviews or focus groups.
Data Sources:
Surveys: Collect quantitative data on participant experiences, satisfaction, and perceived outcomes.
Assessments: Measure specific skills or knowledge areas before and after program participation.
Program Records: Track attendance, participation rates, and other relevant metrics.

3. Selecting Evaluation Criteria
Evaluation criteria are the standards against which program effectiveness will be assessed. Criteria may include specific outcome measures, participant satisfaction ratings, or improvements in knowledge or skills.
Example Criteria:
Percentage increase in academic grades among participants.

Improvement in social-emotional skills as measured by standardized assessments.
Participant satisfaction ratings based on post-program surveys.

4. Establishing a Timeline and Budget

A well-defined timeline and budget are critical components of an effective evaluation plan. The timeline should outline key milestones and deadlines for data collection, analysis, and reporting. The budget should account for costs associated with evaluation activities, including personnel, data collection tools, and analysis software.
Example Timeline:
Month 1: Define evaluation goals and questions.
Months 2-3: Develop data collection tools and protocols.
Month 4: Conduct data collection.
Month 5: Analyze data and prepare evaluation report.

5. Data Analysis and Interpretation

Once data is collected, it is essential to analyze the results systematically. Quantitative data can be analyzed using statistical software to identify trends, relationships, and significant changes. Qualitative data should be coded and analyzed thematically to identify common patterns and insights.
Quantitative Analysis:
Conduct statistical tests to compare pre- and post-program outcomes.
Calculate descriptive statistics, such as means and percentages.

Qualitative Analysis:
Identify themes and patterns in participant feedback.
Highlight illustrative quotes that capture participant experiences.

6. Reporting and Dissemination of Findings

The final step in the evaluation process is to report the findings and disseminate them to relevant stakeholders. Reports should be clear, concise, and tailored to the audience, highlighting key findings, implications, and recommendations for future action.

Types of Reports:

Executive Summary: A brief overview of key findings and recommendations for decision-makers.

Comprehensive Report: A detailed account of the evaluation process, findings, and recommendations, suitable for stakeholders and funders.

Infographics: Visual representations of key data points that can be shared on social media or newsletters.

7. Utilizing Findings for Continuous Improvement

Evaluating program effectiveness should lead to actionable recommendations for improvement. Program leaders should engage stakeholders in discussions about the findings and collaboratively identify strategies for enhancing program design and implementation.

Feedback Loops: Establish mechanisms for incorporating feedback from evaluations into program planning and decision-making processes. This iterative approach fosters a culture of learning and responsiveness.

Challenges in Evaluating Program Effectiveness

1. Limited Resources

Many organizations may face constraints in funding, personnel, and time when conducting evaluations. These limitations can hinder the ability to carry out comprehensive evaluations or implement recommended changes.

2. Resistance to Evaluation

Some program staff or stakeholders may resist evaluation efforts, viewing them as intrusive or unnecessary. Engaging stakeholders early in the evaluation process and emphasizing the benefits of evaluation can help mitigate this resistance.

3. Complexity of Outcomes

Evaluating programs aimed at at-risk youth often involves complex, multi-faceted outcomes. Isolating the effects of a specific program from other external factors can be challenging. Utilizing mixed methods and a robust evaluation framework can help address this complexity.

Case Study: Evaluating a Youth Mentoring Program

To illustrate the principles of program evaluation, consider the case of a hypothetical youth mentoring program aimed at improving academic performance and social-emotional skills among at-risk youth.

1. Program Overview

The mentoring program pairs at-risk youth with trained adult mentors who provide guidance, support, and encouragement over the course of a school year. The program includes weekly meetings, goal-setting activities, and skill-building workshops.

2. Evaluation Goals

The evaluation aims to assess the program's impact on: Academic performance (measured by grade point averages).

Social-emotional skills (measured through standardized assessments).

Participant satisfaction (measured through post-program surveys).

3. Data Collection Methods

Pre- and Post-Assessment: Administer standardized assessments to participants at the beginning and end of the program to measure changes in social-emotional skills.

Grade Tracking: Collect academic performance data from school records before and after program participation.

Surveys: Distribute satisfaction surveys to participants at the end of the program to gather feedback on their experiences.

4. Data Analysis

Analyze grade point averages using statistical methods to identify significant changes.

Calculate improvements in social-emotional skills based on pre- and post-assessment results.

Summarize participant satisfaction ratings and identify common themes in qualitative feedback.

5. Reporting Findings

The evaluation team prepares a comprehensive report highlighting:

Increased average grade point averages among participants.

Positive improvements in social-emotional skills, with specific areas of growth identified.

High levels of participant satisfaction, with feedback suggesting areas for program enhancement.

6. Recommendations for Improvement

Based on the evaluation findings, recommendations may include:

Increasing the frequency of mentoring sessions to provide more consistent support.

Incorporating family engagement activities to involve parents and guardians in the mentoring process.

Expanding the program to include additional skill-building workshops focusing on study techniques and emotional regulation strategies.

Conclusion

Evaluating program effectiveness is a crucial component of any initiative aimed at helping at-risk youth. It allows organizations to assess their impact, ensure accountability, and promote continuous improvement. By employing robust evaluation frameworks and methodologies, such as logic models and mixed methods approaches, programs can gather valuable insights into their effectiveness and make informed decisions about their future direction.

Ultimately, the goal of evaluation is not merely to assess success or failure, but to foster a culture of learning and adaptation that enables organizations to better serve the youth in their communities. Through ongoing evaluation and the willingness to adapt based on findings, programs can enhance their effectiveness, ensuring that they provide meaningful support to at-risk youth and help them realize their full potential.

Chapter 15: Creating a Sustainable Future

Introduction

Creating a sustainable future for at-risk youth requires a comprehensive and integrated approach that considers the unique challenges they face and the resources available to support them. Sustainability in this context involves not only the longevity of programs and services but also the development of resilient youth who can thrive in their environments. This chapter explores strategies for ensuring that programs supporting at-risk youth are sustainable over the long term, focusing on community engagement, collaboration, resource mobilization, and adaptive practices.

Understanding Sustainability in Youth Programs

1. Defining Sustainability

Sustainability in the context of youth programs refers to the ability to maintain and enhance the program's effectiveness over time while adapting to changing circumstances and needs. This includes ensuring that resources—financial, human, and material—are available and effectively utilized to support ongoing activities. It also involves creating systems and structures that promote resilience and growth among youth.

2. The Importance of Sustainability

Creating sustainable programs is crucial for several reasons:

Long-Term Impact: Sustainable programs can provide ongoing support to youth, helping them develop the skills and resources needed to navigate challenges and achieve their goals.

Community Resilience: Sustainable programs contribute to the overall health and resilience of communities, fostering a supportive environment for all youth.

Resource Efficiency: Sustainability ensures that resources are used effectively, reducing waste and maximizing the impact of funding and

efforts.
Equity and Inclusion: Sustainable programs can better address the diverse needs of at-risk youth, promoting equity and inclusion in access to resources and opportunities.

Strategies for Creating a Sustainable Future

1. Building Strong Community Partnerships

Collaboration with community stakeholders is essential for the sustainability of youth programs. Engaging local organizations, businesses, schools, and families can provide additional resources, expertise, and support.
Identifying Partners: Conduct a mapping exercise to identify potential community partners who share a common vision for supporting at-risk youth. This may include nonprofits, educational institutions, local businesses, and government agencies.
Creating Collaborative Agreements: Establish formal agreements that outline the roles and responsibilities of each partner, ensuring that all parties are committed to the program's goals and sustainability.
Leveraging Resources: Collaborate with partners to share resources, such as funding, facilities, and expertise. For example, local businesses can provide mentorship, internships, or financial support, while schools can offer space for program activities.

2. Engaging Youth and Families

Involving youth and their families in program planning and decision-making is crucial for fostering ownership and commitment to sustainability. Programs should prioritize creating a culture of engagement that empowers participants to contribute to their success.
Youth Leadership Opportunities: Establish leadership programs that allow youth to take on roles in program planning, implementation,

and evaluation. By giving youth a voice, programs can ensure that their needs and perspectives are reflected in services.
Family Engagement Initiatives: Create opportunities for families to participate in program activities and decision-making processes. This can include family workshops, advisory boards, or regular communication channels to share updates and gather feedback.
Feedback Mechanisms: Implement systems for youth and families to provide input on program design and implementation. Surveys, focus groups, and suggestion boxes can help gather valuable insights and promote a sense of ownership.

3. Diversifying Funding Sources

A diverse funding portfolio is essential for the long-term sustainability of youth programs. Relying on a single funding source can create vulnerabilities; therefore, programs should explore multiple avenues for financial support.
Grants and Philanthropy: Research and apply for grants from government agencies, foundations, and philanthropic organizations that support youth programs. Tailor proposals to align with the funders' priorities and demonstrate the program's impact.
Corporate Sponsorships: Approach local businesses for sponsorship opportunities, offering them visibility and recognition in exchange for financial support or in-kind contributions.
Fundraising Events: Organize community fundraising events, such as charity runs, auctions, or benefit dinners, to engage the community and raise funds for the program. These events also provide an opportunity to raise awareness about the program and its impact.

4. Implementing Evaluation and Continuous Improvement

Sustainable programs are built on a foundation of evidence-based practices and continuous improvement. Regular evaluation helps identify successes and areas for growth, enabling programs to adapt to changing needs.

Data Collection and Analysis: Establish a robust system for collecting and analyzing data on program outcomes, participant feedback, and community needs. Utilize both quantitative and qualitative methods to gain a comprehensive understanding of the program's impact.

Reflective Practices: Foster a culture of reflection among staff and stakeholders, encouraging them to regularly assess program activities, outcomes, and challenges. This can be facilitated through team meetings, feedback sessions, and structured debriefs.

Adapting to Change: Be open to modifying program components based on evaluation findings and community feedback. Flexibility is key to ensuring that programs remain relevant and effective in meeting the needs of at-risk youth.

5. Promoting Advocacy and Awareness

Raising awareness about the challenges faced by at-risk youth and advocating for supportive policies is crucial for sustainability. Programs can engage in advocacy efforts to garner community support and influence systemic change.

Community Awareness Campaigns: Develop campaigns to educate the community about the issues facing at-risk youth and the importance of support programs. Use social media, local events, and community forums to raise awareness and promote dialogue.

Policy Advocacy: Engage in advocacy efforts aimed at influencing local, state, and federal policies that impact at-risk youth. This may involve working with policymakers, joining coalitions, or participating in advocacy training.

Building a Movement: Create a network of supporters, including youth, families, and community members, who are passionate about advocating for at-risk youth. This network can amplify voices and create a collective impact.

6. Fostering Resilience Among Youth

Sustainability also involves empowering at-risk youth to develop resilience and self-efficacy, enabling them to navigate challenges independently and thrive in their environments.

Life Skills Training: Incorporate life skills training into program curricula, covering areas such as financial literacy, conflict resolution, communication, and goal-setting. Equip youth with the tools they need to succeed in various aspects of life.

Mentorship and Support Networks: Provide access to mentorship opportunities that connect youth with positive role models. Mentorship can foster resilience by offering guidance, encouragement, and support in overcoming obstacles.

Promoting Positive Mindsets: Encourage youth to adopt positive mindsets and self-beliefs through programs that focus on growth mindset, self-compassion, and goal-setting. Building a sense of agency and self-worth is critical for their long-term success.

Case Study: A Successful Sustainable Youth Program

To illustrate the principles of creating a sustainable future for at-risk youth, consider the case of the "Empower Youth Initiative," a community-based program focused on providing holistic support to at-risk youth in an urban environment.

1. Program Overview

The Empower Youth Initiative offers a range of services, including academic tutoring, life skills workshops, mental health counseling, and mentorship. The program aims to empower youth to overcome barriers and succeed academically and personally.

2. Building Community Partnerships

The initiative began by engaging local schools, businesses, and nonprofit organizations to create a collaborative network of support. Key partnerships were established with a local university for tutoring services, mental health organizations for counseling, and local businesses for mentorship and internship opportunities.

3. Engaging Youth and Families

The program actively involved youth in the planning process by forming a youth advisory board. Family engagement initiatives included workshops that educated parents about available resources and ways to support their children's development.

4. Diversifying Funding Sources

The Empower Youth Initiative successfully secured funding from various sources, including grants from foundations focused on youth development, corporate sponsorships from local businesses, and community fundraising events. This diversified funding portfolio provided financial stability for the program.

5. Implementing Evaluation Practices

The initiative implemented a comprehensive evaluation plan to assess program effectiveness. Regular surveys and assessments were conducted to measure participant outcomes and gather feedback for improvement. Data-driven decision-making allowed the program to adapt its services based on participant needs.

6. Advocacy and Awareness

The Empower Youth Initiative engaged in advocacy efforts by collaborating with local policymakers to address systemic barriers faced by at-risk youth. The program also organized community awareness campaigns to educate residents about the challenges youth face and the importance of support programs.

7. Promoting Resilience

The initiative incorporated resilience-building components into its programming, offering life skills training, mentorship opportunities, and mental health support. By empowering youth with the skills and support needed to navigate challenges, the program fostered a sense of agency and self-efficacy among participants.

Conclusion

Creating a sustainable future for at-risk youth is a multifaceted endeavor that requires collaboration, community engagement, and a commitment to ongoing evaluation and improvement. By building strong partnerships, diversifying funding sources, and actively involving youth and families in program design, organizations can ensure that their initiatives are effective and resilient.

Moreover, fostering resilience among youth and advocating for supportive policies are essential components of creating lasting change. As stakeholders come together to support at-risk youth, they can build a foundation for a brighter and more equitable future, ensuring that all youth have the opportunity to thrive and succeed. Through a collective commitment to sustainability, we can create an enduring impact on the lives of at-risk youth and the communities they inhabit.

www.ingramcontent.com/pod-product-compliance
Lightning Source LLC
LaVergne TN
LVHW082249150826
845677LV00009B/1586
* 9 7 9 8 2 3 0 8 5 2 0 2 5 *